HUMANIMAL

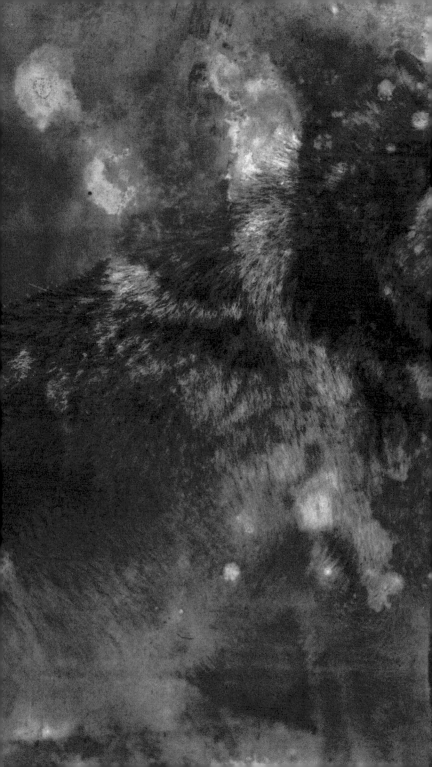

HUMANIMAL

A PROJECT FOR FUTURE CHILDREN

BHANU KAPIL

KELSEY STREET PRESS 2009

KELSEY STREET PRESS

2824 KELSEY STREET BERKELEY, CA 94705

TEL [510] 845-2260 FAX [510] 548-9185

INFO@KELSEYST.COM WWW.KELSEYST.COM

DISTRIBUTED BY SMALL PRESS DISTRIBUTION

[510] 524-1668 OR [800] 869-7553

DESIGN AND COMPOSITION BY QUEMADURA

PRINTED ON ACID-FREE, RECYCLED PAPER

IN THE UNITED STATES OF AMERICA

FOR

THELONIOUS ARJUN RIDER

AND

ROHINI KAPIL

They open up a body that is a lesion in the tissue of words and discourses and the network of powers.

ALPHONSO LINGIS, *Abuses*

That girl has had aberrated physiological patterns all her life—a very slender, flattened, ribs-down pattern. When I was working on her, I was pulling her back from her unique pattern. I was changing a unique but very poorly operating girl to a normal pattern of a woman who could no longer look in the mirror and know that she was unique. I was afraid to say to her, "You are beginning to look like other people." This was what I wanted to say, but I realized that that was the wrong thing to say. [Transcribed remarks on a photograph]

IDA ROLF, *Rolfing and Physical Reality*

This work is based upon the true story of Kamala and Amala, two girls found living with wolves in Bengal, India, in 1920. My source text, the diary of an Indian missionary, Reverend Joseph Singh, was first published in 1945 as a companion text to *Wolf-Children and Feral Man*, a book of essays by the Denver anthropologist Robert Zingg. In the jungle, on a Mission to convert the tribal population, Singh had heard stories of "two white ghosts" roaming with a mother wolf and her pack of cubs. He decided to track them. Upon discovering the "terrible creatures" to be human, he killed the wolves and brought the children back to his church-run orphanage, the Home, in Midnapure. For the next decade, he documented his attempt to teach the girls language, upright movement, and a moral life. Despite his efforts, Amala died within a year of capture, of nephritis. Kamala lived to be about sixteen, when she died of TB.

In 2004, I traveled to Midnapure with the French film-making company, Mona Lisa Production. As part of a documentary on human-wolf contacts, they wanted to film me conducting my research for this book. Thus, in India, I found the graves of the two girls. I found a ninety-eight-year-old woman who recalled their howling. I found a tree in which Kamala had been photographed reaching out to grab the tail of a cat. I found the room the girls were kept in. I found the overgrown garden of the Home with its crumbling brick wall. I found the grandson of Joseph Singh; it was he who placed the blurry photographs, which sections of this work are written from, in my hands.

HUMANIMAL

There are two spaces in which I took notes for feral child-hood. I am not sure if childhood is the correct word. The first space was a blue sky fiction, imagining a future for a child who died. The second space was real in different ways: a double envelope, fluid digits, scary. I was frightened and so I stopped. There were two kiosks like hard bubbles sell-ing tickets to the show. A feral child is freakish. With all my strength, I pushed the glass doors shut, ignoring the screams of the vendors inside, with a click. I clicked the spaces closed and then, because I had to, because the glass broke, I wrote this.

HUMANIMAL 1

BLUE SKY FICTION FOR A FUTURE CHILD.

Balled up, her shaven head and spine visible through her skin, the wolfgirl was a singular presence, almost butter-yellow against the granular fabric of the Kodak paper. When she died, it was Easter, the hot dry month before monsoon. Bowing to custom, the priest covered her face with marigolds, soaked the stems with olive oil then lit a match.

Behind the graveyard was a church, intensely white in the pale pink day.

Behind the church was the jungle.

At the edge of the jungle was a seam, a dense shedding of light green ribbons of bark. A place where things previously separate moved together in a wet pivot. I stood and walked towards it in a dream.

Her eyes were grim, intensely clarified against her charred skin, as she looked up. Above her, the trees were dense with a dark green fruit I could not identify. In the minutes before capture, the girl reached up, her arms criss-crossing rapidly beneath the bleached, low-hanging vines of the perimeter. She was wearing a white cotton dress shredded at the sleeve and hem.

When I developed the film in New Delhi, the x-ray of a marine skeleton was superimposed upon her left arm. Her elbow as thick as a knot. I said it was cartilage—the body incubating a curved space, an animal self. Instead of hands, she had four streaks of light. An imprimatur, she saw me and flinched.

HUMANIMAL 2

A MATRIX OF FLUID DIGITS. IMAGES OF

CHILDREN IN THE UNDER-WORLD.

AN ALPHABET TO O, A KIND OF MOUTH.

1. The humanimal sky is copper like lids. Retrograde stars litter this intimate metallic curve above the jungle. Can you see it?

A. All the branches stir in their silver. Like a liquid metal—the jungle. For her, the girl—tentacular. Does the skin crêpe, where her fingers are too wet, trailing in the river? This is what a child does, as in fairytales. This is walking. I want to. All branches fear life. It pushes and pushes: life. Out to the tips where the color is. Does this happen in Asian forests? Does this tree say yes, damaged by its yes, to phloem—the food to the lips? Of the branches where the leaves are and thus a leaf girl—leaping from branch to branch in her dream of being a girl and not this, this other disastrous thing?

2. Like automata, the trees rise up in rows, mechanically. Because it's January, we don't see scat or paw marks or tufts of blue hair caught in the low-lying branches. This is tracking but the wolves—wild black dogs with elongated torsos —are deeper in. The District Forest Officer lifts a luminous skin from a termite mound with the snout of his rifle and holds it up to show me. When I reach out to gather another section of the skin, he stops my hand with his. When I ask if snakes are active at this time of year, he says: "Oh no, no, madam, the Indian anaconda is not a problem at this time of year. Not at all. No problem!" Nevertheless, we return in short order to the jeep with footage, only, of a rudimentary perimeter in which giant insects have constructed conical temples from the moist, ochre earth beneath the

trees. I want to stay, but the film-makers are stubbing out their cigarettes in the dirt. I didn't know the jungle would be red.

B. I want to stand up but I can't do that here. They would know I am a wolf by my sore hips, the look in my eyes. At the edge of the garden was a line of blue chalk. My mother was crouching there, waiting for me in her dark coat. In the dream, I walk towards her and she stands up. She opens up her coat like two wings and I step into her cloth heart, her cleft of matted fur.

3. The girl, I cannot retrieve even one foot from her small leg. A tendon. A nail. One eye. I saw her grave in a city where the edge had been. In your city, or where you grew up, was there an overgrown scrubland? Was there a tree? Imagine a dark tree, like a lemon tree, its fruit still green, studded with parrots. The edge of sal: lemon and banana plantings intermixed with the regular blue. It is blue leaves at night and brown, yellow or doubly green by day. But it was day. But

blue. I put my hand on her grave and waited, until I could feel the rhythm, faintly, of breathing. Of a cardiac output.

c. Mist rose in cubes. With hard fingers, they tore strips from my spine. All blonde-black fur. All hair from a previous life.

4. Feral children are fatty, complex, and rigid. When you captured the two children, you had to brush the knots out of their hair then scrape the comb free of hard butter. Descent and serration. No. I don't want to ask primal questions.

5. Kamala slips over the garden wall with her sister and runs, on all fours, towards the complex horizon between Midnapure and its surrounding belt of sal. The humanimal mode is one of pure anxiety attached to the presence of the body. Two panicked children strain against the gelatin envelope of the township, producing, through distension, a frightening shape. The animals see an opaque, milky membrane bulging with life and retreat, as you would, to the inner world. I am speaking for you in January. It is raining. Am-

niotic, compelled to emerge, the girls are nevertheless re-absorbed. I imagine them back in their cots illuminated by kerosene lanterns. I illuminate them in the colony—the cluster of residences, including the Home—around St. John's. No. Though I've been there, it's impossible for me to visualize retrieval. Chronologies only record the bad days, the attempted escapes.

D. I was almost to the gate. I was almost to the gate when a hand reached out and pulled me backwards by my hair, opening my mouth to an O. The next day, I woke up with a raw throat. The cook gave me salt in warm water. I waited until she was gone and then I bit it. I bit my own arm and ate it. Here is my belly, frosted with meat. Here are my eyes, bobbling in a tin.

6. It's Palm Sunday and Kamala, with the other orphans in a dark, glittery crocodile, walks from Home to church. Her two arms extend stiffly from her body to train them, to extend. Unbound, her elbows and wrists would flex then

supinate like two peeled claws. Wrapped, she is a swerve, a crooked yet regulated mark. This is corrective therapy; the fascia hardening over a lifetime then split in order to re-set it, educate the nerves.

E. The cook fed us meats of many kinds. I joined my belly to the belly of the next girl. It was pink and we opened our beaks for meat. It was wet and we licked the dictionary off each other's faces.

7. Is this the humanimal question? No, it's a disc, transferring light from corner to corner of the girl's eye. Like an animal tapetum. The way at night an animal. Animal eyes, glinting, in the room where he kept her, his girl, deep in the Home.

8.i. Where is the future child? Curled up with wolves, subred, the wolfgirl's eyes reflected light. She was seven when her Father found her, coiled in a den. A tall, extremely handsome Father, sidetracked from his Mission—dressed in black despite the heat—caught her in a bed-sheet, and wrote: "I cut a hole and removed her from the cave."

8.ii. Your scars lit up then liquefied. Lucidly, holographically, your heart pulsed in the air next to your body; then my eyes clicked the photo into place. Future child, in the time you lived in, your arms always itched and flaked. To write this, the memoir of your body, I slip my arms into the sleeves of your shirt. I slip my arms into yours, to become four-limbed.

9. In Midnapure, in a back room, a jute bed is converted to a low cot. Strapped in, the wolfgirl turns her face from the window. Does the Home have windows? It's 1921, mid-November, and I can't find her sometimes, on the other side of everything. Stresses of light—I don't know how to change them, these amounts. This is absurd. I write on a piece of paper all morning, then fold it in two.

10.i. This is the humanimal project. All the fingers are still inside the hands. A mother-to-be's hips ache. In the forest behind her hut, the birds are so red, the wrong red, against the bed of green. A forest is a bed for animals. When the rains come each June, these animals make nets in the upper branches, suffering nightly, twitching, from an incomplete, lunar darkness. It's the time before electricity. Those are not birds. They are wolves, switching their glossy brown tails in the heat. As custom dictates, the woman gives birth, then places her newborn girl on a shawl beneath a tree, massages her with coconut oil, and leaves her there to sun. Lit up like that, the baby is vulnerable, naked thus flesh-like, fleshed like prey, but flailing—four legs in the air like pink, elongated stars.

10.ii. I am not interested in animals. Return to the work as memory. Say it is a wolf becoming a girl, the action in re-verse.

10.iii. They strapped her down to the limited table where a knife spun in a jar of blue water. There were marigolds and red thread sewn into the white cotton curtains. Oranges lined up on the sill. Like a spell. Like an angel, the priest fed Kamala from a coil of linen, squeezing water into her open mouth. She spat it out and so the doctor came with his packet of edges. Dipped one into the glutinous foam and began. Her arms first. The thick dorsal hair, ashy. Her legs first and then her skull.

11. The air is pink by seven and there is Naxalite graffiti on the tree trunks of the stupid jungle. These are sal trees in West Bengal. A girl facing sal, 1920; it's still Orissa. These are notes for a separate project. But I'm here and I'm trying to see it, eighty-four years later: the humanimal trait. How she, through a density I can't manage but overlaid by a separate forest. I can't manage her forest and say it is sal, but a century on the sal is regulated.

12.i. How she moved, through sal. But these new trees are new, too young to be hers. The de-forest. The way land is always settled, gives up and then there are mercies. A planting. People—Britishers, then Hindi speakers from the north—swerving sal with their agricultural systems. In this third space, the trees make a sort of heart, a red space filtered loosely—pink light—to the rim. Gleaners—nomads, from Bhutan and present-day Orissa—are pushed back each year into the darker, more rigid sections of the jungle. Behind the film-makers, I walk through alternating bars of sunlight and shadow, luxuriating, nowhere. Footsteps. The police escort assigned to our party, panting, says: "Madam!

Please tell them, they are not understanding. Are you Indian? Please talk to them on this point. The tribals have started up again. They know you are here, with your film equipment and all this. Madam, are you France? Are you American? I think you are born in a different country. Am I not right?"

12.ii. Walking through a jungle lit by blue paper. When they filmed the jungle they made pockets of soft blue light. "Walk more slowly, like you're thinking. Again! One more time. Yes! Now . . . very naturally, very casually, look left, into the trees, as if you're looking for wolves."

13. But how she went into her garden, an indivisible red, and was not seen by her mother when a passing wolf picked her up in her quick beak. The mouth of the wolf was the sharp pink O that covered her and kept her still as they—the girl and her new, animal mother—crossed into the green. Nearer to the sal, I can see the tree trunks are red-orange, dusty, and that the lines they make are clear. I walk for hours between the rows as she did not. This is a different place and I want to know what happened, to the trees.

F. The cook scraped vernix or matte and saw a shape beneath the fats, suitable for reaching. "Your arm." "Your hand." "Your left." And sliced them free of the wild animal.

14.a. The earth is red and shiny on this January night. I have wandered away from a shot. I crouch down next to the man, who is barefoot, trousers rolled up to the knee, navy blue nylon windbreaker zipped to the chin. He is kneading a baby-sized loaf of red clay, scooping water from a bucket with his cupped hand, by candle-light. In rudimentary Bengali, I ask him what he's doing. He's curt: "Dushu." "What is it for?" "The river." The documentary translator, a Calcutta native and film student from Paris, R., has followed me to tell me they're ready. I ask her to ask what dushu is. In a monotone, clearly tired from the late shoot, she translates: "Sarasvati. She is our mother and we give her back to her mother. The river is our mother. I take her to the river."

14.b. In the morning, I go back to the village and see a tiny army of goddesses, some sun-baked, some still wet and some painted, delicately, with necklaces of white and red

Krishan, my father, was born in India in 1937, ten years after Kamala died. This is a photograph of scar tissue, to represent a deep cut in his leg from a street beating. What is a street? Here, the flesh is healed over, repaired by natural processes. If the image, the excess rectangle, extends to the next page, mark it black. This scar doesn't fade; it doesn't melt, over time, into a skin.

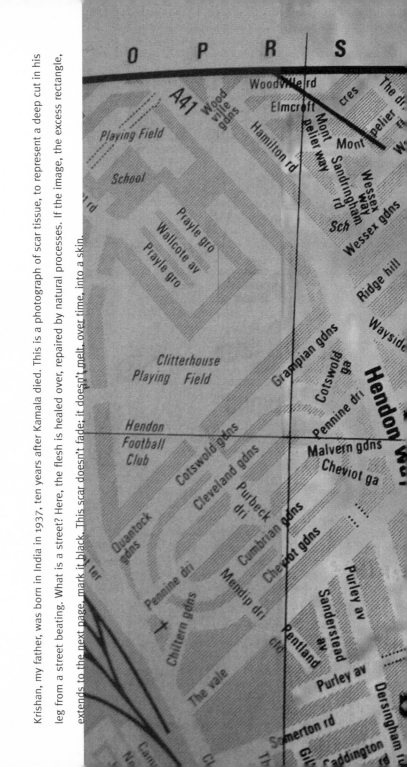

dots. Some of the heads are separate to the torsos and when I come upon him, the sculptor has one of these heads in his left hand. With his chin, he gestures to another head and to the leaf, like a bowl, with a white paste in it. "Really?" He shakes his head in a figure of eight, and I set to work massaging the paste into the faces then putting them aside to dry.

15. Coming over a ridge, Joseph saw two pale animals, their heads hanging down and thick with brown dreadlocks. They were drinking from a river with a pack of wolves. A twig snapped underfoot as Joseph strained to look but at that moment, the animals fled, in one sharp curve, back into the green. At night, the animals came once again to drink. In his hide, Joseph shivered. He could not see them clearly but he knew they were there. In the moonlight, the wolves and their companions were whitish, with eyes that shone when they turned towards him, mildly, reflexively. Blue.

G. Wet, wet, green, green. I mix with them and prosper. Sticky then my mother licks me clean.

The nest is brown. Best is brown next to yellow. Best is blue then brown. Best yellow. Where will the sun go when it is finished? I ask my mother. I put my lips against her skin and drink. Her milk is white and then the sun goes in the ground. Because my mother does, she does so every night. We watch her disappear and then we disappear. Blue as blue then brown then green then black.

16.i. In the bedroom, he tried to feed her with a copper spoon, a mineralized utensil to replenish her blood. He made her eat, watching the pink food—a kind of semolina pudding mixed with jam—pool in her mouth. Her mouth was an O and with his fingers he tried to press her gums and teeth together. "*Eat.*" In the time I am writing of, villagers from the settlement of Midnapure came regularly to the orphanage, lining up at the gate to catch a glimpse of the two jungle children. For a few minutes a day, Joseph's wife, the Home's Mother, let them in and they swarmed to the room where the youngest girl was failing. They watched her fade and jerk in her cot, the spittle coming down over her chin. From these stories, I constructed an image of the dying girl as larval; perennially white, damp and fluttering in the darkness of the room.

16.ii. "She was buried in the churchyard of St. John's Church, Midnapure, on the twenty-first of September, 1921. Her death certificate ran as follows: This is to certify that Amala (wolf-child), a girl of the Rev. Singh's Orphanage, died of nephritis on September 21, 1921. She was under my treatment. September 21, 1921. sd/-s.p. Sabadhicari. Indian Medical Service." —Joseph Singh.

16.iii. In Midnapure, I met the grandson of Dr. Sabadhicari. As the film-makers asked him to describe the stories his grandfather had told him, I sketched, in my notebook, the emerald green, rusted spiral staircase partially illuminated in the dark hallway behind him. Suspicious of our cameras, Dr. Sabadhicari retold the tale his grandfather had told him, of the two feral children, from the front step of his door. "What is this for? Are you American?"

17. I substitute images for events, my humanimal preroga-
tive. Thus, here are the legs, wrapped in cotton wool to pre-
vent them from breaking; for the shocks absorbed in trans-
port, in the act of getting here at all.

18. A doctor came from Midnapure with a vial of herbal med-
icine and a knife. Wizardly, grandmother-like, he stuck out
his chest and stomach and said: "Where are they?" The
girls. The doctor strung a knife above the cot where one girl
lay on the white sheet. Her face was wet. The cook soaked
the water up with a square of cotton and the Father backed
out of the room. In the garden, the sky hung down in vio-
let sections like a torn net and the Father stood there, be-
neath it, calling out to the angels in their dominion. When
the youngest girl died, the doctor came out into the garden
and sank into a wicker chair. It was a chair from Nepal, the
edge of the region. The Mother brought the doctor a plate
of buttered chicken and chilies, which he ate quickly and
sloppily, like a dog.

19.i. A light blue rain fell in intervals upon the upturned faces of wolves.

19.ii. Each feral moment is valuable. Magically, the legs slip out of their sockets deep in the hips. Milky photographs fell out of my skirt and I crouched to collect them by the grave.

20. Translating her story from Punjabi, I wrote this: "When it started to rain, the banyan tree outside the girl's room, where she lay in a profound coma, shook. Then the rain stopped and there was no wind but the tree was still going hard, rattling. I heard something growling in the branches. A small white snake was lying on the roots. The tree shook into the night and at midnight, when it stopped, visitors from the nearby village were allowed to see the girl. I went with my mother, a woman whiter than any white person we know. She had brown-green eyes. My mother placed a gift of oranges on the bed. There was an herbal doctor in the room and he took one of the oranges and placed it on the girl's belly. As soon as he did this, blood began to trickle out of the girl's belly-button and also from

the orange. A painting on the wall tilted of its own accord and we ran from the house, screaming. By morning, the girl was dead."

H. A white smoke fills the compound. Children gallop in the garden of the Home. I want my mother. With one crack in the stuff of her she was gone. But these are my hands. But the sun burns my hands. Kill the sun.

21. Slow, wet orange sun and such a bright full moon over the jungle's horizon. Looking down from the lodge, there are long saffron scratches where the sun has caught a mineral vein. Notes for film: "A girl emerges from a darker space into the upper rooms of the jungle. Blurry photographs/transitions of light." How does this sentence go into animals? Notes for an animal-human mix: "Reaching and touching were the beginning actions."

22. I wake up stiff, wrapped in a quilt, on the wicker chair. The sun is a pale green disc in the white sky. I dreamed last

night that I was crawling on the floor with a circus acrobat from the 1940s. He was Chinese and his eyes were ringed with black lead. As if in a trance, I left my seat in the audience and danced with him. It was a dance based upon the movements of a black panther and a white eagle. We crossed them. This was mating deep inside the market. We danced until we were markets.

23. The humanimal conquest is a moonlit capture. The moonlight illuminates the termite mound where the wolves have hollowed out an underground cave with their beaks. Sub-red, animal wolves and human wolves curl up with their mother, in sequence, to nurse. When the babies fall asleep, the mother slips out into the jungle. As she crosses the blue clearing, Joseph cocks his gun and aims, the culmination of weeks of hunting. There is a dazzling break in the darkness.

24. The trees rise up in rows. A red disc shines through the thin curtain but the trees look spiky through the nylon grid. I came here to write. Can feeling grow here? In waves—a memory of the ocean bed it once was? An animal flowers in the elements. It grows wings. A cat with wings alights on

the doorstep, as if to say, I'm off. I don't need your food anymore. These are notes for a separate project, in which the jungle is a "kind of foreign language extracted from the maternal language, on the condition that the sounds of phonemes remain similar."

25.i. The film-makers have hired the local folkloric theater, a troupe funded by the state's Marxist council, to re-enact the capture of a girl by a wolf. They don't need me in this scene, so I lie down behind the drummers, three elderly men pounding cotton-wrapped mallets on drums as huge as them. I lie on the ground beneath the music. A lean, bearded man in a wolf costume is holding a girl in his arms. R. sarcastically says: "They want her to act as if she's almost dead. And the wolf is carrying her home to eat." R. is smoking a Gauloise and as I watch, she throws it on the dirt and grinds it down beneath her boot. Army boots, long black hair to the waist, jeans, ridged yellow fingernails. I can tell she thinks this is dumb. Indeed, later, back at the lodge, she says: "Do you mind?" Smoking, she jabs the air with her cigarette, trailing ash over the azaleas: "I wish it was just you and me. I want *hazard*. I want to travel everywhere in India. Not just here. There is no CHANCE in this film." But below us, in the parking lot, the film-makers are packing their lamps into leather satchels with hard backing. One of them looks up at us and waves. R. and I look at each other and burst into giggles. A boy opens the door but we can't stop laughing. "Chai?" We take the tiny glasses of steaming ginger tea from him and resume our exchange. When the boy comes back to get the glasses, R. says: "What do you want? What are you looking at? Get out of here, you damn bloody fool."

25.ii. Of the sixteen children who were born, only seven— six boys and a girl—survived into childhood proper. One of the boys pushed the girl off the roof and then there were six. My father was the second oldest, and though I am not sure if the image—my aunt Subudhra falling upside down to her death, a kite's slim rope still bound to her wrist and wrapped twice around her knuckles—is relevant to the story I am telling, it accompanies it. In the quick, black take of a body's flight, a body's eviction or sudden loss of place, the memory of descent functions as a subliminal flash.

1. With nets and sheets, they made a canopy over my body, and I curled up inside the air. With teeth and earth, they made a net around my body, and I curled up inside my hair.

26.i. In the photograph, a girl climbs a tree, reaching out to grasp the tail of a cat. I climbed that tree, disturbing a true sphere with its knotty fingers, elongated thigh muscles, and blue eyes brightly lit even in a darkened room. I wrote then stopped. What stopped my hand?

26.ii. The Reverend Joseph slipped an ankle-length black dress over his head and his gun over that; the strap dug into his left shoulder as he transgressed a wild space of gold, smashed grasses and transparent mountains, to reach the caves. The cave was littered at its entrance with bones. The porters gave him their coarse, white woolen shawls and he threw them over their forms. Two girls. "I saw them first." Flailing then rigid then soft.

27. A woman left her daughters beneath a tree then tiptoed back to town. A wolf woke up deep in the tree. A girl was a speck on the ground, so the wolf picked her up in her hairy beak and flew off into the trees. When the girl was found in a milky cave, they shot her mother the wolf and tore her out of her hair. Then there was tea. Sugary tea with milk sucked from a rag, and they bound her pelvis in cotton. There is a formal photograph that survives in anthologies of this period: the wolfgirl seated, center front of a row of orphans, at Joseph's feet. The eyes of the good children do not waver. When the photographer shouts from under his black cape—1, 2, 3—our girl is the only one who looks up at a raven passing overhead, shaking her head like a dog on a rope, to howl. "Owowwoow." Joseph kicks her hard, his face completely blank for the camera, but it is too late. It is 1924. The photograph will be blurry. Two faces blossom from one thin neck.

J. When she came for me, I was ready. Limp in her teeth, where she had me by the scraw. From the threadless, dusty stretch between my mother's house and the edge of the world. Into a channel the color of fevers, white, white, white then green. I saw a white-pink face with ash in its forehead lines. It was a woman, sitting in a tree. One big eye saw me then shut and we continued. I saw a turtle flying from branch to branch, a white, hooded snake in her yellow beak. I saw three thousand eyes switch on and off. They saw me and I saw them. Nobody followed us but when the Reverend found us, he wrote: "Remembering without sound." Then he put down his pen. To listen. "What a dog is." "Lop lop." "Trees and dogs, which no one can change."

28. Though I waited, there was no memory of a cross—the lifting up, loss and going—that I was so interested in when I first began to think of her, the feral child. In a white dress, like an insect, she waited with the others for the meat. Biscuits. A bell.

K. I had a tail. I have a hymn. My frayed blue hymnal I left in the box by my cot and the Father smacked my side with a wand. I wore a skirt. I had a dress. A grey skirt with maroon cotton stitching on the hem. But there was milk in my mouth and so I drank it. With my mother, there in the curve of the cup. A red cup and I drank it. When I wept, she licked me clean, wetting down my hair with her tongue. No. It's Friday. I must still be a child.

29.i. Perimeter space transfuses moonlight. The trees filtrate it. Is it filtration, or is it pre-history? Is it ambience? To cull the sal for export, the British erased sections of the forest, then re-planted it like a Norfolk copse, brutally. Linearity is brutal. Yet, now, the jungle is more luminous and spacious than it would have been naturally. It's early, about five a.m. Staring at the perimeter from the verandah, I warm my hands on a glass of ginger chai. Here, I have a private view of a corrupt, humanimal landscape, a severed fold.

29.ii. The legs: as a child, my father ate butter straight from the cow. Once, when his mother caught him red-handed at the churn, she beat him to blood with a bamboo cane. My father, a tiny, wiry boy, was smoking by age seven. Switching the cows home through fields of rape, his chest level with the sharp yellow blossoms. Barefoot, his feet resembled those of a goat's: hard, rough, and smooth. Were his cells even then beginning to pulse? Pulse and break up/proliferate? What is a membrane? It's the light on the field in 1947, by which I can barely see a boy. He slips out of the field, disappearing into a settlement of shacks. Dusk. I can smell the country fires, bread popping and burning on dry, freshly lit cakes of dung. The sun is slipping over the roof of the tall building across the street. In a few minutes, India will be illuminated.

30. Crimson azaleas spill over the rail and onto my knees. No filming today and so I'm writing. The humanimal document is a machine that produces redness by itself. In Normandy, as a child on a school holiday, I saw a giant pink moon rise over the brown curves of the field. Remembering that moon, I put it in India. I put it inside the jungle like the light given off by certain animals even in the dark. Self-illuminate. And watched it rise. Have you ever seen pink moonlight? It is frightening. It is a cousin to shadow, just as a wolf is to a dog.

31.i. In the shadow of the church, in the Home, Joseph took Kamala's hair in his fist and cut it off, close to the skull. His wife swaddled the girl in a dress with thick cotton bandages beneath it, where she'd scratched her skin. Joseph held her elbows together behind her back and, with his other hand, bathed her forehead with water at the font. This was October: the month and the time. It was morning, as it is now. In a transition of light—late morning—I went to the church. In the atrium, a chipped, porcelain angel was suspended over a bank of chairs made from Saigun wood and carved (the legs) with leaves. Because it was not quite Three King's Day, strips of red, green and yellow aluminium foil were still strung loosely above the pews, fluttering and rotating in the breeze coming through the windows. The Christmas decorations extended to the dark space where the altar was, and they glittered there. I was happy. I was happy to see the creamy, butter-yellow walls of St. John's at Midnapure warping a little with the light bouncing off the stars and snowflakes. Leaving the film-makers to interview the prelate, Reverend Singha, who had unlocked a cabinet to look for Kamala's death certificate, I went into the garden. It was a field. A group of boys were playing cricket but when they saw me, they dropped their bats. "Show me where the graves are." "I'll show you, didi! I'll show you! Aap baar se? Are you from outside?" I took a sticky paw in each of mine and, propelled, found myself in the ruins behind the church. Here, the ground was hard, nude, and three tombs were positioned in a rough semi-circle. Approaching the nearest one with the suddenly quiet children, I read its partially eroded inscription, then wrote it down: "Sacred to the Reverend Frederick Fisher, M.A., Chaplain of the Bengal establishment, Susanna Anna, his wife, and Philip, their youngest son who perished by the hands of the Rebels [sic] off Singhee Rampore. July 1853. God moves in mysterious ways. His wonders to perform." "Madam," said the Reverend Singha, who had followed me out, "please come away from this place. Get away, children! No! *I'll skin you alive* ... Madam, please. These children are very dirty. You could be having infection and all of this."

31.ii. My father's legs were covered with silver pockets where the flesh had been scooped out then varnished to a high sheen. My father herded goats, supporting his family, for a time, in its entirety. His own father had died of an opium overdose; I don't think then exactly, but later. My father's mother built a shelter out of tin and wood and straw and mud for the children. The second oldest child, my father, sold goat's milk and tended the animals in the world of fields that extended in all directions for hundreds of miles. A twelve-year-old, illiterate boy, my father was standing in a field when he had a vision. He said: "I suddenly knew that when I grew up I would be a teacher in England. I said, 'I will go to England and teach English to the English'." And he did. He dragged himself out of the field and into the sky.

L. "Ud: Ashud/Medicine. Doo: Dudh, Milk. Bhā: Bhāt/Rice. Moor: Muri/Parched Rice. Māng: Māngsa, Meat. Foo: Phul, Flower. Hut: Hāth/Hand. Dim: Dim/Egg. Khel: Khalera/ Toy. Pān: Pān/Betel Leaf. Zo: Jal/Water. Maz: Mach/Fish. Ain: A-inah/Mirror. Fok: Farak/ Frock. Chui: Churi/Knife. Bag: Baghān/Gar-

den. Cho-Ghoi: Chota Gharu/Timepiece. Joot:
Juta/Shoe.—Kamala's words, with Bengali equiv-
alents and English equivalents, as recorded by
Joseph on December 1924 when he wrote, ob-
serving her during a bout of fever and dysentery:
"One peculiarity was especially noticed during
this illness: her tongue became active, and she
commenced talking in a fashion that amazed us
all immensely. Though the words were broken,
yet she expressed herself in a wonderful way."

32. The compound was a salt square, white or bad to the far
wet green lines. Above the lines, in the creases between wall
and "bag", were pomegranate bushes. The cook left a dish
with a bloody sauce outside them, glancing up from her
work, until, like one big eye, Amala crawled out to get it. The
"mang". She hooked the meat in her palm, scratching the
dirt with the fingers of her left hand as she ate, a weak dis-
play behavior. Then she slept, for hours, beneath a spiky
level that was an element, roughly cube-shaped; a bank of
green; an entrance. When she died, they found a bed there,

threaded with Sunday ribbons she'd gathered like red silk straw from the garden, where they'd slipped from the orphans' hair. Sensible orphans in the roaring sun running past the bushes to the well. Nearer to the house, the cook set traps for snakes and fried them. She cooked them and she put them on a plate. When I was a child returning to London after a year in India, the children on my street asked me if it was true. "Did you eat snakes for breakfast?" As a joke, I said yes and for a summer or so read books in my garden, shut out from their games: "little black pig," "Paki snake-eater," and so on. When I grew up, I wrote about the blood-stream of a child as intermingling with that of an animal. Within an environment, the glide path of this child was soundless. When conditions fluxed, I built a flux gate. I made a cut in the trees and let her go.

33. Animal myths, like that of a human consumed by a wolf, depend upon a girl. She loses her way one day, disoriented by the gathering shadow at the edges of a copse. Something glints deeper in, and she pursues it, imagining it to be candlelight in the window of a hut. But it's a tooth. No.

I can't see her to completion, opposing myth which is life-like: pre-ecdystic, a transformative state. In this re-telling, the girl is gone forever and I'm not sure how she eats. I'm not sure how she survives the night.

34. Accused by an orphan of biting, Kamala is called into Joseph's study where he bites her back. Beats her with a bamboo wand, then pricks her in the palm with its tip. A teacher, he wrote, in 1927: "Kamala learned to identify herself with the children. On the third of December, she was standing at the dining table when the table was being laid for tea. Mrs. Singh, finding her there, gave her a biscuit. She ran to the children, and all the children flocked around the table, expecting to get a biscuit each. Mrs. Singh scolded them for this coming in before the tea bell rang, and one by one they all left the dining room. Kamala put her biscuit on the table and went away."

35. I wanted to write until they were real. When they began to breathe, opening their mouths in the space next to writing, I stopped writing. I imagined all the children in the sky,

part of the monsoon wind, the molecules of rain circulating from ocean to land and back again. A pressure. A loop. In this way, I wrote until the children left the jungle, the country itself, their families of origin, and time. I saw how they changed time. But the next day, I switched on my computer and read this: "PHNOM PENH, Jan 19, 2007 (Reuters Life!) —A Cambodian woman who went missing in the jungle for eighteen years before being found last week is struggling to adapt to life as a human and wants to return to the forest, police said on Friday. 'She prefers to crawl rather than walk like a human', said Mao Sun, a district police chief in the jungle-clad northeastern province of Rattanakiri where the girl's family lives. 'Unfortunately, she keeps crying and wants to go back to the jungle', he said. 'She is not used to living with humans. We had to clothe her. When she is thirsty or hungry, she points at her mouth', he told Reuters by phone. The girl, called Ro Cham H'pnhieng, went missing as an eight-year-old along with her cousin when they were sent to tend cows near the border with Vietnam. Villagers believed they had been eaten by wild animals until a girl was caught last week by a logging team as she was trying to steal some food they had left under a tree. With blackened skin and hair stretching down to her legs, she was unrecognizable apart from a scar across her back that allowed her father to pick her out. After eighteen years in the wilderness, police said she was able to say only three words: father, mother and stomach ache. Her father said: 'She is a bag of bones'."

M. I looked into Amala's eyes in the photograph but she looked away and began to cry. She destroyed the paper. She killed her face.

36. In the aeroplane from London to Kolkata and in the jeep to Midnapure, I put my knib on the page and let motion wreck the line. My notes were a page of arrhythmias, a record of travel.

37. A girl is a dot arising in space, and then the girl after that, and the next. Viral, schizophrenic, the two girls shook in the garden, and then in their beds like photographs. In the first days of their captivity, they screamed for their

mother, then stopped. Dehydrated, they sucked tea from rags. Accepting nourishment like this was a primary act of human culture. Hopeful, their Father brought them home. No. They were home and then they got sick, unable to tolerate the food they were given. What is digestion? It is the ability to assimilate proteins. What is a protein? I don't know. Is everything inside the body a kind of liquid, a way of taking information from site to site?

N. I saw their tiny black eyes squinting through the fence. I saw the tiny mirrors sparkling on their hems. Were they wolves?

38. In the photograph, her flesh floats next to her in the black and white air; it doesn't adhere. Her bones are delicate, slightly too long to be a human child's and coated finely, with wet fur. I know about the body because I held it in my hand. In the photograph. It was January. Joseph's great-granddaughter brought me a glass of water, but I didn't drink it because it wasn't boiled. It wasn't clean.

39.i. "I saw two white ghosts, their hair hanging down in knots to their knees, drinking from the water with three wolves; another wolf, the mother, was hanging back from the bank. When she saw me, she growled and in an instant, the wolves and the two ghosts had disappeared into the trees."

39.ii. "Close after the cubs came the ghost—a hideous-looking being; but the head was a big ball of something covering the shoulders and the upper portion of the bust, leaving only a sharp contour of the face visible, and it was human."

40. The air is filled with Bengali, French, and English. In the District Forest Officer's, P. R. Chakroboty's office, we drink boiling hot, intensely sweet milky tea from tiny, grimy glasses as we wait for our film permit to be processed. The D.F.O. is wearing a threadbare khaki sweater with a hand-knitted white scarf wrapped tightly around his neck. An orange, red, and yellow hand-towel covers the back of his

chair. There's a large square of emerald green felt beneath the glass surface of his desktop and the telephone cord is still wrapped in its original cellophane packaging. The D.F.O. has sindoor, a scarlet powder, freshly packed into the deep parting of his flattened, oily hair, and as he outlines to us the risk of filming a "natural forest" during a period of Naxalite "activity" —"How can I say this, sirs? Please to understand, you are foreigners. You are white and, as such, your safety ... I advise. You should write your story here in Midnapure. We have a very good lodge ..." —the red seam flakes, scattering on the ridge of his nose. The film-makers are persistent, indifferent to local politics, and soon we are off. As night approaches, the sun becomes a dazzling cube and red earth sticks to the trees where it's kicked up by our jeep. We stop to look for tracks but it is January; the wolves are hibernating in pink underground tunnels lit by lanterns. There is a risk but not a visible one. On the contrary, the damp earth smells intensely sweet, the air is green and we are here in our white shirts to cull an atmosphere; to scrape color and sound and light into jars.

o. I took a leaf from the Home to dry it, to make a piece of paper with three raised seams.

41. Unable to assimilate the sulphites Dr. Sabadhicari gave her, the youngest wolfgirl, Amala, died of kidney failure on a high cot. Kamala, her sister, though they were not sisters biologically but made sisters by feral life, keened and shuffled for many days at the perimeter of the Home. During this time, Joseph took a photograph of her climbing a tree and extending her arm towards the leg of a cat. I found this tree and climbed it. Then I found the room where Amala died, and opened the door. There was a man inside the room. He was about twenty-five years old, dressed in a white dhoti, and cross-legged on a cot, reading a tattered book covered with newsprint in the Indian fashion. When he saw me, he grinned and leaped up to stand on the bed. Reaching up to a sack hanging from a hook on the ceiling, he retrieved a glass bottle filled with cloudy water. Passive to India, dazzled, I did not resist him when he poured some water into his cupped palm and put it to my mouth. "Ganga-jal. Paio."

I drank it, holy water from the Ganges, and backed out into the garden, to spit.

42.i. On Sunday, October 17, 1920, Joseph found the wolves and wrote: "But I failed to realize the import of the circumstances and became dumb and inert. In the meantime, the men pierced her through with arrows and she fell dead. After this, it was an easy job. I collected four big sheets from the men and threw one of the sheets on the ball of children and cubs and separated one from the other."

42.ii. The doctor breaks Kamala's thumbs then wraps them in gauze.

43. Notes for a companion text. The coast of Wales. Your legs were a brown and silver frame to the day: bony, skinny really, and smashed-up looking beneath a coat of coarse, black hair. The sand was white, as were the other holidayers. I felt bitterly the contrast of our own exposed skin against the blueness of the sky and the waves. Your legs were frankly an embarrassment: visible chunks of flesh taken

from your thighs and shins at another point in history. Mummy's bright yellow sari with its schizophrenic border of green and black zig-zags, and so on. Only in the water were you and I a family: colorless, wavy and child-centered. Invisible to the eyes of the other families. Do you remember? A wave bobs us up, higher than the person with the camera. Embedded in the dark, silver cream of the Kodak paper, you're like a brown rectangle with a black dot for the mouth and two brown arms. I am a brown dot and one brown arm, obscured by iridescence; your singular, limbed progeny.

o. And into the sky. I saw her slip between the bars then into a bird. The cook crossed herself and spilled water on the doorstep to the compound to see it. A tree. Shaking on a windless day. I ran out into the air wrenching myself from twenty red arms: the orphans, the cook. What was happening? Then a bird flew over us, a black bird like a raven or a crow, and dropped a white dot from the sky. It fell on me.

44. Imagine a body emitting red worms, thick as fingers and as long.

45.i. In a companion text, intrusion functions as an organizing principle. As an adult, for example, I take pleasure in the well-ordered house with the furry dog on the floor and the leg unaffectedly balanced on the mantelpiece. It's a human leg. It's art.

45.ii. My father's body, in those first fifteen or sixteen years of his life, changed from a liquidy, peeled thing—constantly re-opened spots of tissue—into another kind of body. The scarring process is regenerative in that you're healed, but now you look different. My father's legs, for example, pooled with a silvery protein that hardened into long ovals and other shapes on his shins and thighs, though his feet were beautiful. Perfect, long-toed and white, as I recall. In the hospital, I massaged his legs, something that distinguished me from the other grown children in the reservoir of breath, that public bedroom. Pressing two rows of points, the spleen and the liver, I waited until he was asleep before

I left. In the basement cafeteria, I ordered tomato soup, which I drank from the bowl, cupping my hands to bring it to my mouth as I gazed out at the trees and the rain and the darkening, indigo sky. My father died young, in his fifties, though the doctor told me privately that his body was clearly ravaged by the debilitating effects of poverty, early malnutrition and the multiple musculo-skeletal traumas that he appeared to have sustained as a child. "On the contrary, Miss Kapil," he said in a theatrical whisper next to the bed, "it is a miracle he lived this long. He should really have died as a child." "You should go home, ducks," said the nurse, and I did, passive to the ward's routines.

45.iii. As a child, I was waiting just outside my father's office, kicking my legs on a chair as I read *Bunty*, my weekly comic. I was waiting with a tall black boy of about twelve, already six feet tall. "What did you do?" "Nuffink." Without warning, both incredibly fast and in slow motion, my father came out of his headmaster's office with a cane. Within moments, the boy was writhing on the carpet, doubled up— "Please, sir!" Without thinking, I stood and ran through the corridors of the school. I have a vivid memory of a frieze of gold and silver spray-painted coffee beans, arranged to form the spirals of a galaxy on a huge sheet of black paper. It must have been many pieces of paper, stapled together. I forget.

O.

47. I want to make a dark mirror out of writing: one child facing the other, like Dora and little Hans. I want to write, for example, about the violence done to my father's body as a child. In this re-telling, India is blue, green, black and yellow like the actual, reflective surface of a mercury globe. I pour the mercury into a shallow box to see it: my father's right leg, linear and hard as the bone it contains, and silver. There are scooped out places where the flesh is missing, shiny, as they would be regardless of race. A scar is memory. Memory is wrong. The wrong face appears in the wrong memory. A face, for example, condenses on the surface of the mirror in the bathroom when I stop writing to wash my face. Hands on the basin, I look up, and see it: the

distinct image of an owlgirl. Her eyes protrude, her tongue is sticking out, and she has horns, wings and feet. Talons. I look into her eyes and see his. Writing makes a mirror between the two children who perceive each other. In a physical world, the mirror is a slice of dark space. How do you break a space? No. Tell me a story set in a different time, in a different place. Because I'm scared. I'm scared of the child I'm making.

48. They dragged her from a dark room and put her in a sheet. They broke her legs then re-set them. Both children, the wolfgirls, were given a fine yellow powder to clean their kidneys but their bodies, having adapted to animal ways of excreting meat, could not cope with this technology. Red worms came out of their bodies and the younger girl died. Kamala mourned the death of her sister with, as Joseph wrote, "an affection." There in a dark room deep in the Home. Many rooms are dark in India to kill the sun. In Midnapure, I stood in that room, and blinked. When my vision adjusted, I saw a picture of Jesus above a bed, positioned yet dusty on a faded turquoise wall. Many walls in India are

turquoise, which is a color the human soul soaks up in an architecture not even knowing it was thirsty. I was thirsty and a girl of about eight, Joseph's great-granddaughter, brought me tea. I sat on the edge of the bed and tried to focus upon the memory available to me in the room, but there was no experience. When I opened my eyes, I observed Jesus once again, the blood pouring from his open chest, the heart, and onto, it seemed, the floor, in drips.

49. I met Mahalai in Godamuri, where we were, to film a troupe of Marxist actors dressed as wolves, jungle animals, and children. I hung back in the village as the film-makers constructed a bamboo cage and R., the translator, persuaded a mother to undress her daughter, cut her hair, and dress her in a makeshift cloth diaper. I walked away from this scene and asked a woman rolling a cigarette if I could rest in her garden. Smiling, she said yes and offered me papaya from a stainless steel bowl at her feet. In Bengali. And I ate it. I ate language. As Mahalai, dexterous and blank, pinched finger after finger of tobacco to construct, in seconds, tight-looking bidis to add to the white pyramid be-

fore her, she sang. Her song was familiar and it made me want to cry. I was exhausted. Mahalai got up and poured some tea from a terracotta jug into a smaller clay cup and brought it to me. She was a wiry, tiny woman somewhere between forty and sixty with a long, oiled, grey-black braid down her back. She watched me drink, and then we talked in the place where her Bengali and my Hindi crossed. Then, without warning, she took my cup and set it on the ground. She grabbed me, shoved my head into her lap and started to massage my scalp. Her husband came home, carrying a bucket of wet clay and disappeared into their hut. My whole body felt rigid but then, abruptly, I submitted to her touch. When I woke up, I was covered with a shawl and someone, Mahalai, had covered me with tiny, pink-orange blossoms from the pomegranate bush at the gate. Was there a gate? R. found me and shook her head. I was officially somewhere on the edges of the story. A light rain set in and we returned to the lodge for a late dinner of fried fish, yoghurt and rice.

50. My own mother told me another story of possession, with its attendant fable of exorcism, as a child. There was

a girl of nine in the village of Nangal who had been over-taken by an evil spirit after a failed pilgrimage to the Kali temple in the hills above her home. Kali had come to her that night and stuck out her long, black tongue. The girl told her mother the dream, but by nightfall she had a fever and by the next night, was nearly gone. Each night the priest fed her purgative herbs, and at midnight, she was permitted visitors. "A few days later, my friend was dead, and I remember when we played by the river. Our cousin-brothers buried our dolls in the sand, but the rains came before we could dig them up. I cried and cried."

o. Citron-yellow dots collect and scatter. A silver sky collapses in folds upon the canopy. The grid divides then divides again. When the girl crawls out of the broken jungle, she's soaked in a dark pink fluid that covers her parts. Fused forever with the trees of the perimeter, she can't. The branches fill her mouth with leaves. I can't breathe.

51. What are your primal images? The man walking knee-deep across the outdoor swimming pool, a candle cupped in his palm? The ever-present running water at the corner of each black frame? Rain? Dogs? The color indigo or midnight blue next to gold. Your mother or father lighting the candles for Friday night dinner? Are you from another country? I wasn't expecting it, the immediate response to a temperature. My blood let out a deep sigh. Is it wrong to feel immediately at home in India, where, if its citizens knew you felt that way, would laugh you out of the house? But I felt it. Two minutes out of Kolkata airport, driving to the city, I breathed in the air in deep gulps, releasing the chemicals of permanence.

52. Seven years ago, I walked to the University of Colorado from my rented apartment on Goss. There, in the dark library, I closed my eyes and let my right hand drift over the stacks. Where my hand stopped, I opened my eyes, chose a book at random and read this: "October 17 Captured; Oct. 28 Leave Godamuri; Nov. 4 Arrive Midnapore; Nov. 10 Loin-

cloth stitched on; Dec 16 Noticed sleeping on overlapping position; Dec 10 Only sound peculiar cry in dead of night. 1921: Jan 3 Can see in dark. January. They try to escape, morose, bite Roda. To end of January, complete dislike for everything human (A. also) Lips tremble; Sept. 4, A. falls ill; Sept. 12 Worms evacuated; Sept 21 A. dies, K. will not eat or drink, wants to be with corpse; Oct. 8 K. smells all places A. used to frequent, pants in sun, tongue out; Nov 25 Improves, becomes old self—via massage; Dec 2 Comes in room where Mrs. S. is, takes red toys in mouth; 1922: March 4 Can stand on knees whenever she likes without pillow; March 6 Finds dead chicken, runs into bushes and devours it, understands endearments; May 10 Wall bracket exercise begun; Sept 15 K. smells meat at 70 yards—growls; Dec 24 Fear of fire; 1923: Sept. until Sept., 1923: (during first 3 years) no laugh or smile; 1924: March 11 Says 'soo' for saraju; 'toom' for 'toomy'='I am'; Nov. 18 Locked out of inner compound; extremely frightened, takes refuge in haystack. Tries to open door by force, fails. I called to her ... instead of shunning my company, (she) now sought it."

53. Jungle space is zero space. How could you stay? Imagine a girl in her childhood dress, fluttering at the edge of the jungle, pinned by it yet living. On February 22, 1924, Joseph wrote: "Kamala pulled out a red frock. Mrs. Singh asked her why she wanted this frock. She at once replied in a drawn-out expression, 'L-a-l' (the Bengali word for 'red'). This was sufficient to show she understood what she meant."

54. I place a mirror in a cave, in a garden, on a leaf. It is a tiny, circular mirror of the sort used in the embroidery of chests and hems. In this way, I can train or invert an obsidian frame to hold light, make a face clarify. Today I saw a face dormant in the darkness of the jungle. Coming near and kneeling, I saw it was the open face of a child. Future child, I slip one hand under the curve of your skull and another beneath the vine of your neck.

55. Beneath the glorious canopy, I see a zero continuously crossing the line where it thins. Red next to green: a vibra-

tion. Something loosening inside a color and it is a similar desire that makes her cross. Is it? The edge of the jungle is not the place where the line shifts the most. That is deeper in where the caves are, pink with bones.

56. Her mother walked to the edge of the village and placed her in the roots of a tree where the sounds of human activity were still clearly audible. Her pulse rose but her mother left her, which is an ancient story. Near night, she stood; the child stood, undying, already partially metallic in her effort, her resiliency, and went in. Perhaps she crawled. This is a text to keep her safe and so I followed her into the jungle. Worms, flowers. I stayed awake all night and watched her while she slept, deflecting predators with my intensity, my pressure just before appearance. Nevertheless, I did sleep and inevitably, when I woke up, she was gone.

57. The tropical modern is breakable, a fragile globe enclosing the jungle, reflecting back the green. When it breaks, the green is, thus, muted, intensifying the pink of feathers, eyes, clothing and flowers. Heat doesn't break it. The sky

does. No. I don't know what perturbs then banishes environment forever, but it does. I wrote another book like a blue lake then drained it, to write from a dip. I am writing to you from depression, from a body of black cloud through which a bird's shadow passes, like a knife.

58. A girl returns to her jungle home, shedding her dress at the perimeter. No. There's a citron-yellow flare of thunder and simple, pure red blossoms hang in the rough black air. The girl is lying in a nest, endangered yet coiling like a sea-creature in her sleep. I stay awake all night on the tip of love, a test of sight's force. How come you love her too? Do you have a child? Do you want a baby? These are the wrong questions but they pass the time. They make a body real. This is a text to do that. Vivify.

o. I've exhausted the alphabet. But I'm not writing this for you.

59.i. With nets or sheets, shawls and ropes, they get her and bring her down. For humanimals, this is a destiny that cannot be averted. Each time she crosses, in truth or fiction, she breaks the tracery of delicate glass threads that marks the border. A border is felt in the body as fear and sometimes ... no, I cannot speak for her now. Here, there are mango trees wavy with light green vines. Each crossing disrupts the gelatin envelope, producing tracks. With a stick, Joseph lifts a strand of long black hair where he finds it curled over the orange fruit.

59.ii. Flexion, a dominant feeling like surge. This is revision, a re-telling of planar space. In the enchanted forest, a finger strokes the forearm of the reader reading of a tree in flower. He opens the flower to see a human eye, which is muscular: a motif moving of its own accord—animate, but with a future inviolate to perception and with its memories intact.

60. Reaching and touching as the beginning actions, reorganized in time as desire. On our last night in Kolkata, in the hotel corridor carpeted with pale yellow wool, I said goodnight to the film-makers, suddenly shy. As the aeroplane banked above the pink-orange ocean the next morn-

ing, I understood that the humanimal moment occurs most powerfully at dawn, when the eyesight adjusts to the light of the upper rooms of the jungle. I understood it in the air. As the plane descended to Oman, I felt the one to ten worlds contracting: red fish hanging in a butcher's window; hotel bed sheets, coffee with milk, cinnamon and sugar— then London, where the sun at seven was a wet fire. In the morning, from the sky, I saw Atlantic floes pulsing imperceptibly in the darkness below. As the plane descended to Denver, I took a dry leaf, a banana leaf with three raised seams, from its place in my book and crumpled it, crushed it really, onto my leg through my skirt.

ACKNOWLEDGEMENTS

With gratitude to Mona Lisa Production, Lyon, France, especially Quincy and Pierre-Francois, for the incredible adventure of filming in India. Without you, I would never have seen the jungle flooded with blue or encountered the word "humanimal."

With gratitude to Reema, Professor Ghose, the Singh family, and Reverend Singha for access to the world of Midnapure: for your translations from Bengali into Hindi and English, and for opening your homes to me.

With gratitude to Anne Waldman and Lisa Birman for inviting me to teach in the Naropa University Summer Writing Program. Mona Lisa Production found me through you. Thank you, most of all, for making a nest for writing that is also a nest for hybrid figures of all kinds.

With gratitude to my undergraduate and graduate students at Naropa University and Goddard College, for the conversations that link biology and architecture until the grid begins to pulse. The grid of narrative.

Thank you to Melissa Buzzeo and Andrea Spain: our trined conversation on healing, exhaustion and mutation, at the limit of a species field. You helped me to form grids out of jungles and concepts; to create a space in which a book could fail, then re-grow, like a body.

Thank you to Rohini Kapil for giving me the language of the tropical modern and for designing/altering the image of our father's imaginal limb overlaid with fragments of a London map.

With gratitude to Kelsey Street Press, for an enduring support of experimental writing by women of all variations. Thank you, in particular, Amber DiPietra and Hazel White, for our conversations in passing towards a body forming itself in time, which is a book.

And thank you to the editors of the magazines in which forming excerpts of this project have previously been published: *mem, plan b, notenoughnight, Bombay Gin, Denver Quarterly, XCP, President's Choice, Thuggery & Grace, How2,* and *Jubilat.* Earlier versions have also appeared in the Belladonna Books pamphlet series, as well as the Norton Anthology *Language for a New Century*, edited by Tina Chang, Natalie Handal, and Ravi Shankar.

Finally, I'd like to thank the following people for their assistance in the permissions process: Aurelia Alvarez Urbajtel, Jacklyn Burns, and Scott Cutler.

I gratefully acknowledge the following publishers and persons who generously granted me the permission to make use of materials from the following works:

COVER: Manuel Alvarez Bravo, *Of Vices and Virtues: Tobacco*, 1932. Gelatin silver print, $6^{15}/_{16} \times 9^{9}/_{16}$ in. Copyright © Colette Urbajtel. Reprinted by permission of the J. Paul Getty Museum, Los Angeles.

PAGES 20–21: Rohini Kapil, digital image, 2008. Reprinted with permission of Rohini Kapil.

PAGES 44–45: Joseph Singh, photograph of Kamala and Amala asleep, 1921. Reprinted by permission of Scott Cutler at the Centennial Museum. University of Texas, El Paso.

Excerpts throughout from *Wolf-Children and Feral Man* by Robert M. Zingg and J. A. L. Singh. Copyright 1939, 1941, 1942 by Robert M. Zingg; renewed © 1970 by Emma K. Zingg. Reprinted by permission of HarperCollins Publishers.